Paul the prisoner

Story by Penny Frank
Illustrated by Eric Ford

THE LION
STORY BIBLE

52

OXFORD · BATAVIA · SYDNEY

The Bible tells us how God sent his Son Jesus to show us what God is like and how we can belong to God's kingdom.

Rome was the most important city in the time of Jesus — and of his special follower, Paul. The emperor of Rome ruled the world.

Paul knew that he must take the good news about Jesus to Rome before he died.

You can find the story of how that happened in your own Bible, in the book of Acts, starting at chapter 25.

Copyright © 1987 Lion Publishing

Published by
Lion Publishing plc
Sandy Lane West, Littlemore, Oxford, England
ISBN 0 85648 777 5
ISBN 0 7459 1797 6 (paperback)
Lion Publishing Corporation
1705 Hubbard Avenue, Batavia, Illinois 60510, USA
ISBN 0 85648 777 5
Albatross Books Pty Ltd
PO Box 320, Sutherland, NSW 2232, Australia
ISBN 0 86760 562 6
ISBN 0 7324 0117 8 (paperback)

First edition 1987, reprinted 1988
Paperback edition 1989

British Library Cataloguing in Publication Data

Frank, Penny
Paul the prisoner. – (The Lion Story Bible; 52)
1. Paul, *the Apostle, Saint* – Juvenile literature
I. Title   II. Ford, Eric, *1931 –*
226'.60924   BS2506.5
ISBN 0-85648-777-5
ISBN 0-7459-1797-6 (paperback)

Printed in Yugoslavia

Library of Congress Cataloging in Publication Data

Frank, Penny.
Paul, the prisoner.
(The Lion Story Bible; 52)
1. Paul, the Apostle, Saint – Juvenile literature. 2. Missions – Italy — Rome – History – Juvenile literature. 3. Rome (Italy) – Church history – Juvenile literature. [1. Paul, the Apostle, Saint. 2. Bible stories – N.T.] I. Ford, Eric, ill. II. Title III. Series: Frank, Penny. Lion Story Bible; 52.
BS2506.5.F73 1987   226'.60$9505
86-18520
ISBN 0-85648-777-5
ISBN 0-7459-1797-6 (paperback)

The followers of Jesus in Jerusalem were very worried.

Paul, their friend, who went everywhere telling people the good news about Jesus, had been arrested.

His enemies had made trouble, and now he was in prison, in a place called Caesarea.

But that did not stop Paul telling people about Jesus.

He talked to the guards. He talked at his trial. He talked to the governor and even to the king.

'I have done nothing wrong,' Paul said. 'I have only told people that Jesus, who was killed, is alive again.'

4

'It is a matter for your own people to decide,' said the governor. 'You will have to go to Jerusalem.'

'Although I am a Jew, I am also a citizen of Rome,' Paul told them. 'I claim my right to be judged by the emperor.'

'Then we shall send you to Rome,' the governor said.

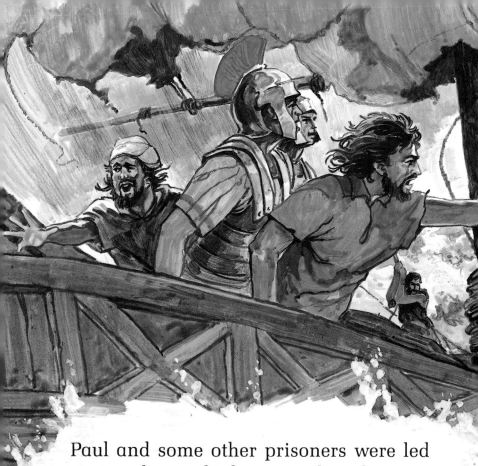

Paul and some other prisoners were led on to a boat which was sailing for Rome.

Paul was glad to have his friend Luke with him. There was a soldier in charge of them.

When the boat had been sailing for some time a terrible storm started.

The wind howled around the boat. It
blew the waves high, over the decks. The
boat was tossed up and down on the
sea.

The prisoners were afraid. So were the
sailors.

'We'll all be drowned,' they screamed.

But Paul knew that they were not going to be drowned. God had told him that they would all arrive safely. He shouted to the men to trust God.

At last, when daylight came, they saw an island nearby.

But suddenly there was a terrible crash. The boat had been thrown onto a sandbank. It was hit by giant waves and began to break in pieces.

Clinging to planks torn from the boat, they all jumped into the cold sea and struggled to the island.

They helped each other out of the water and stumbled up the beach. Their clothes were wet and cold. The wind blew the sand into their faces.

Quickly they collected wood for a fire. Some people from the island helped them. They began to dry themselves by the fire.

Paul reached out to put more sticks on the fire. He did not see that there was a snake in the sticks. The people gasped when they saw the snake bite him. They thought he would die.

But Paul just shook the snake off. Nothing happened to him. They knew, then, that God was keeping him safe.

When winter was over, it was time to set sail again for Rome. They went on board another boat.

This time the weather and the winds were just right and they arrived safely.

There were people in Rome who already knew about Jesus. When they heard that Paul was coming, they went down the road to meet him.

Paul was so pleased to find that he already had friends in Rome who followed Jesus.

The soldier in charge of the prisoners took Paul to a house.

'You have not hurt anyone, or stolen anything,' he said, 'so you can stay in this house. You will have a soldier to guard you, and you are not allowed to go out. But your friends can visit you.'

So the people who wanted to hear about
Jesus came to see Paul in his house. Paul
enjoyed telling them all about Jesus and
the kingdom of God.

Paul spent much of his time writing letters. He had preached in many towns, so he had lots of friends. They would be wondering where he was.

Some of his friends had heard only a little about Jesus and God's kingdom. Paul wrote long letters to them.

He told them what was happening to him. He reminded them about how Jesus had died for them and risen to life again. God had given them new lives. Paul was excited as he thought about how different they were now.

Paul chose some of his trusted friends to take the letters. They had to travel by boat and by donkey.

Sometimes they had to walk a long way to reach the people Paul had written to.

When a letter arrived, all the Christians met together to read it over and over again. They wanted to learn all they could about living in God's kingdom.

The Christians took great care of Paul's letters, and we can still read many of them in our Bible. There is even a letter Paul wrote to the people in Rome before he arrived there.

There are letters to people in Corinth, Thessalonica, Galatia, Ephesus, Philippi and Colossae.

And there are letters Paul wrote to special friends — to Timothy, Titus and Philemon.

Paul followed Jesus all his life and
looked forward to going to be with him
when he died. They say that Paul was
killed in Rome because he preached the
good news about Jesus Christ.

That same good news has been passed on to people all over the world for two thousand years.

We are still talking about it today.

The Lion Story Bible is made up of 52 individual stories for young readers, building up an understanding of the Bible as one story — God's story — a story for all time and all people.

The New Testament section (numbers 31–52) covers the life and teaching of God's Son, Jesus. The stories are about the people he met, what he did and what he said. Almost all we know about the life of Jesus is recorded in the four Gospels — Matthew, Mark, Luke and John. The word gospel means 'good news'.
   The last four stories in this section are about the first Christians, who started to tell others the 'good news', as Jesus had commanded them — a story which continues today all over the world.

The story of Paul's trial and voyage to Rome comes from the New Testament book of Acts, chapters 25–28. Thirteen of the New Testament letters — Romans to Philemon — bear his name. They show his deep love and concern for the scattered groups of Christians — 'the young churches'.
   In his very last letter, the second letter to Timothy, Paul looks back on a life spent serving Jesus. He is facing death.
   'I have fought the good fight,' he says. 'I have finished the race. I have kept the faith.'
   Death is even more exciting than life, because he knows he is going to be with Jesus. And ahead lies his reward, 'the crown of righteousness', which God will give each one of his faithful followers on the day when he judges the world.